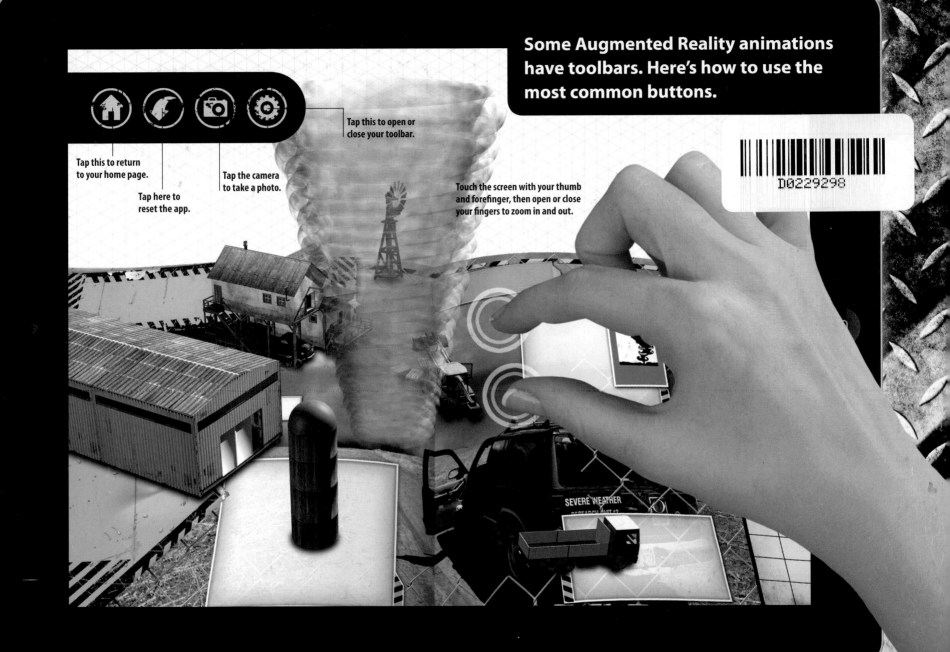

Some Augmented Reality animations have toolbars. Here's how to use the most common buttons.

Tap this to open or close your toolbar.

Tap this to return to your home page.

Tap here to reset the app.

Tap the camera to take a photo.

Touch the screen with your thumb and forefinger, then open or close your fingers to zoom in and out.

D0229298

SEVERE WEATHER RESEARCH UNIT #2

Need some help?
If you've got a problem, check out our website:
www.carltonbooks.co.uk/icarltonbooks/help

WARNING!

THIS IS A CARLTON BOOK

Text, design and illustration copyright:
© Carlton Books Limited 2014.

Published in 2014 by Carlton Books Limited.
An imprint of the Carlton Publishing Group,
20 Mortimer Street, London, W1T 3JW.

A catalogue record for this book is available from the British Library.

ISBN: 978-1-78312-088-8
Printed in Dongguan, China.

Executive editor: Anna Brett
Senior art editor: Jake da'Costa
Design: MWDigital Graphics
Picture research: Ben White
Production: Ena Matagic

Picture credits
The publishers would like to thank the following sources for their kind permission to reproduce the pictures in this book.

Key: t: top, b: bottom, l: left, r: right, c: centre

Alamy Images: 9br; Corbis: /Glowimages: 14-15, /Jeremy Horner: 25t, /Jim Reed Photography: 10-11, /NASA/Roger Ressmeyer: 6-7, /BPPT/Reuters: 25b, /Galen Rowell: 26-27, / Michael S. Yamashita: 22-23; Getty Images: 12, 15tr, 15r, 20, 20-21, 28-29, /AFP: 13t, 16b, 18, 19b, 21, 23c, 26b, /Ingólfur Bjargmundsson: 29, /Mitchell Funk: 23b, /NY Daily News: 14; iStockphoto: 7, 8, 8-9, 17, 19r, 27tr, 18-19, 30-31, 31; PA Photos: /AP: 11t, /AP Photo/Khalid Tanveer: 16-17; Photolibrary.com: 9c, /Warren Faidley: 12-13; Reuters Limited: /Ho New: 24-25; Rex Features: /Sipa Press: 27t; Science Photo Library: /Jim Reed Photography: 11c; US DoD: 13br

Every effort has been made to acknowledge correctly and contact the source and/or copyright holder of each picture and Carlton Books Limited apologises for any unintentional errors or omissions which will be corrected in future editions of this book.

CARLTON KiDS

iStorm

ANITA GANERI

WILD WEATHER AND OTHER FORCES OF NATURE

RESTLESS WORLD

Our planet, the Earth, is a constantly moving and changing world. These changes can be violent and destructive, causing terrible disasters that make the news headlines. Some disasters are caused by extreme weather events, others are the result of natural forces deep inside the Earth.

This photograph of the Earth seen from space shows the swirling storm clouds of a hurricane over the Atlantic.

WIND AND WATER

Hot sunshine, wispy clouds, howling winds, pouring rain and drifting snow all make up the weather we experience from day to day. Our weather happens in the lowest layer of the Earth's **atmosphere**, called the troposphere. The Sun's rays heat the surface of the Earth, which in turn heats the air in the troposphere. The heating is uneven, so the air gets warmer in some places than in others. These differences in temperature make the air move about, creating anything from a gentle breeze to a violent hurricane.

Water plays a big part in the weather. The clouds we see in the sky are made up of water – either billions of small droplets or tiny ice crystals. The water that forms clouds has evaporated from the seas and the land. This water often falls on us as rain, hail or snow. So water constantly moves into the atmosphere and then falls back to the ground. Weather experts call this the water cycle.

PLANET EARTH

Hold the world in your hands and see how the surface is made up of tectonic plates. Then discover where real-life hurricanes and tsunamis have occurred.

WILD WEATHER

Sometimes the movement of the air and the movement of water in the water cycle create extreme, wild weather events. These include **hurricanes**, **tornadoes**, heavy rainfall, **blizzards**, **heatwaves**, **droughts** and thunderstorms.

FORCES OF NATURE

The ground beneath us is a layer of solid rock called the Earth's **crust**. At its thickest the crust is about 60 kilometres deep, so it is very thin compared to the size of the Earth. Below the crust is another layer of rock, called the mantle, which is thousands of kilometres thick. Some of the rock here is actually semi-molten (semi-liquid). Below the mantle is the Earth's core, which reaches temperatures of up to 5,500ºC – that's more than 50 times hotter than boiling water!

The crust is not as solid as it seems. It is cracked into many giant pieces, called **tectonic plates**, which slide extremely slowly over the mantle below. Where the plates meet at their edges, molten rock from the mantle (called **magma**) often forces its way to the surface, forming **volcanoes** that eject **lava** and **ash**. Sudden movements of the plates cause **earthquakes** and if these happen under the sea, they can set off giant waves called **tsunamis**.

Volcanic eruptions are one of the most dramatic signs of the powerful forces at work deep inside the Earth.

CLIMATE AND CHANGE

Climate is the pattern of weather in a particular place and how it varies over a long period of time. For example, a temperate climate brings warm summers and cool winters, with some rain throughout the year. A tropical climate brings hot and humid weather all year round, with heavy rain almost every day.

Over the last hundred years or so, the world has warmed very slightly and climates are beginning to change. This is known as **global warming** or **climate change**. The changes may only be small, but their effects could be huge over the next decades. Some climate experts think that a temperature rise of only 2ºC could cause sea levels to rise and major flooding. This could seriously affect food and water supplies around the world.

INSIDE THE EARTH

crust

mantle

tectonic plate

outer core

inner core

plate boundary

THE EARTH'S CRUST

mountains

volcano

continental crust

ocean

oceanic ridge

continental crust

oceanic crust

two plates colliding

tectonic plates moving apart

one plate moving over the other

upper mantle

magma

magma

magma

mantle

THUNDERSTORM

A bolt of lightning lights up the sky, followed by a deafening clap of thunder – a thunderstorm is breaking! Lightning is made by giant sparks of electricity jumping through the air. Thunder is the noise made as the air expands. It sounds scary, but is not harmful. However, lightning can be deadly.

TOWERING CLOUDS

Thunderstorms begin when warm, moist air rises up through cold air higher in the atmosphere. The warm air is lighter than the cold air, so it floats upwards. As the warm air cools, the water vapour in it turns to water droplets and ice crystals. When there is a lot of warm air, the air keeps rising, forming towering cumulonimbus clouds, which can be more than 10 kilometres high.

Cumulonimbus clouds build vertically as a thunderstorm develops over Maui, USA.

DANGER, ELECTRICITY!

Strong air currents move up and down through cumulonimbus clouds. As they do, water droplets and ice crystals smash into each other. This creates electrical charge on the droplets and crystals. Gradually, a positive charge grows in the top of the cloud and a negative charge grows in the base of the cloud.

Finally the electric charge jumps from the cloud in a flash of **lightning**. The flow of electricity heats the air to about 30,000°C – that's about five times hotter than the surface of the Sun. This makes the air rapidly expand, making the booming sound of **thunder**.

You can track how far away a thunderstorm is by counting the seconds between the flash of lightning and the clap of thunder. Every three seconds you count equals one kilometre.

Cloud-to-ground lightning strikes the city of Hong Kong, China, during a heavy thunderstorm.

CLOUD-TO-GROUND

The electric charge jumps between the base of a thundercloud and the ground below.

CLOUD-TO-CLOUD

Lightning jumps from the base to the top of a cloud, or from the base of one cloud to the top of another.

CLOUD-TO-AIR

Lightning jumps from a cloud to the air around it. This often happens alongside cloud-to-ground strikes.

LIGHTNING STRIKE

Although cloud-to-cloud lightning is the most common, cloud-to-ground lightning is the most dangerous, because it can strike trees, buildings and people.

When lightning hits an object on the ground, a powerful electric current flows through it, causing it to heat up. If lightning hits a tree, the electricity makes the tree's sap boil in an instant, blasting the tree apart. Lightning is actually responsible for starting many forest fires.

People hit by lightning are normally badly injured or killed because they get a giant electric shock. This can cause severe burns and even a fatal heart attack.

A forest fire caused by a lightning strike in Yellowstone National Park, USA.

GROUNDED

Lightning can also damage buildings. Many tall buildings have metal rods on their roofs, called lightning conductors. Because metal is such a good conductor of electricity, it channels the lightning safely to the ground, protecting the building.

Lightning strikes the lightning conductors on the Sears Tower and John Hancock building in Chicago, USA.

TORNADO

A tornado is one of the most extreme weather events on the planet. This violent, funnel-shaped storm spins across the ground, destroying everything in its path. With wind speeds of up to 500km/h, tornadoes smash houses to pieces, hurl cars high into the air and leave a trail of debris behind them.

A tornado tears across the ground in Western Kansas, USA, part of the famous Tornado Alley.

TORNADO

Build a tornado by adding the weather icons in the correct order. Then set it spinning and create a trail of destruction.

COLD DRY AIR	WARM MOIST AIR	STRONG WINDS	HORIZONTAL SPINNING AIR	RISING AND FALLING AIR	STRONG DOWNDRAFT

TWISTING WINDS

Tornadoes often occur where cold dry air meets moist tropical air. This can create massive rotating thunderstorms called supercells. Inside a supercell, strong winds blow in different directions at different heights. Sometimes this makes the air below the storm spin horizontally, level with the ground below.

Powerful rising and falling air currents can tip the spinning air up into the thundercloud, so that it spins vertically. When a strong downdraft pulls this spinning air downwards and out of the base of the thundercloud, a rotating funnel-shaped cloud called a vortex appears. If the vortex reaches the ground, it becomes a tornado!

TORNADO ALLEY

Tornados can happen almost anywhere, but they happen a lot in Tornado Alley: a stretch of the USA running from Texas through Oklahoma, Kansas, Nebraska and the Dakotas. About 700 tornadoes rip through this region each year. Many homes in the area have storm shelters that can withstand a tornado.

SEVERE WEATHER SHELTER AREA

The Tri-State Tornado that ripped through Missouri, Illinois and Indiana, USA, on 18 March 1925, was the deadliest single tornado on record. It killed nearly 700 people and created a trail of destruction 350km long.

STORM CHASERS

Because tornadoes are such violent storms they are difficult for scientists to study. To measure the forces at work inside tornadoes scientists chase after them in fast vehicles equipped with special measuring equipment.

TORNADO POWER

The strongest winds in the world are found in tornadoes. A tornado's strength, or intensity, is measured by the damage it does. Experts grade this intensity, using the Enhanced Fujita Scale. It was invented by Professor Theodore Fujita at the University of Chicago in 1971.

EF SCALE	WIND SPEED	DAMAGE
EF0	105–137km/h WEAK	
EF1	138–178km/h WEAK	
EF2	179–218km/h STRONG	
EF3	219–266km/h STRONG	
EF4	267–322km/h VIOLENT	
EF5	more than 322km/h VIOLENT	

HURRICANE

Hurricanes are massive, swirling storms that start over tropical oceans. The centre of a hurricane, known as the eye, is relatively calm, but the weather surrounding it is wild, with thick clouds, heavy rain and powerful spiralling winds. Hurricanes are called cyclones in the Indian Ocean and typhoons in the Pacific.

A SPINNING STORM

A hurricane starts when a cluster of thunderstorms drifts over the warm ocean around the equator. The warm water heats the air above, causing it to rise very quickly. It then cools to form thunderclouds and rain. As the storm gets bigger, it starts spinning. If the windspeed of the tropical storm increases to around 118km/h it becomes powerful enough to be classed as a hurricane.

A hurricane can measure almost 1,000km across with a circular **eye** up to 100km wide. If a hurricane reaches land, it can cause massive damage, but over land it dies down in a few days. This is because it no longer has a supply of warm, moist air to power it.

Hurricane Frances struck the coast of Florida, USA, in September 2005 causing serious flooding.

The eye in the centre of Hurricane Wilma can be clearly seen in this satellite photograph of it spiralling towards the south of Mexico in 2005.

In October 1998, Hurricane Mitch struck Central America with winds blowing at more than 240km/h and heavy rains that caused catastrophic flooding and lethal **mudslides**.

HURRICANE FORCE

Hurricanes are measured according to how strongly the winds are blowing and how much damage they do when they hit land. Experts rate them using the Saffir-Simpson hurricane scale. A category five hurricane is the most powerful.

CATEGORY	WIND SPEED	STRUCTURAL DAMAGE
1	118–152km/h	Minor flooding along coasts. Little structural damage. Some damage to mobile homes and trees.
2	153–176km/h	Damage to roofs, windows and doors. Some trees blown down. Small boats swept ashore.
3	177–208km/h	Damage to buildings. Mobile homes destroyed. Leaves torn from trees. Serious flooding.
4	209–248km/h	Roofs torn off and walls collapse. Beaches washed away. Large boats swept inland. Severe flooding.
5	Over 248km/h	Buildings destroyed by the wind, some near the coast swept away. Flooding up to 16km inland.

FROM A TO Z

The progress of hurricanes is closely watched, in order to warn people if they are approaching. To make hurricanes easier to identify and track, they are given names, such as Hurricane Emily. A new, alphabetical list of names is started every year. There are separate lists for each region. If a hurricane is particularly damaging, its name is never used again.

STORM HUNTERS

In the USA, 'Hurricane Hunter' aircraft fly into hurricanes to collect data about their strength and direction. To reach the eye of a hurricane the crew have to fly through the towering clouds around it, known as the eyewall. This is the toughest part of each mission as the plane gets tossed around by thunderstorms and powerful winds.

BLIZZARD

Blizzards are deadly snowstorms that combine heavy snowfall with strong winds and biting cold. Snow is blasted along horizontally by powerful gusts of wind that can reach speeds of more than 56km/h. Blizzards can last for more than three hours and they make travelling extremely hazardous.

SNOW HAZARDS

Blizzards occur when two air masses – one cold and dry and the other warm and moist – suddenly collide. The warm air is forced up over the cold air, creating violent snowstorms.

Blizzards can cause serious damage. Heavy snow can bring down power lines, bury cars and trucks, and smash roofs. Cities are brought to a standstill and people are sometimes left without heat, water, food and power. Because blizzards can blow up so suddenly, people may find themselves trapped in their homes, offices or cars.

The extremely low temperatures that occur during blizzards also put people at risk of hypothermia (when body temperature drops below normal) and frostbite (when skin and body tissues freeze). People can die from both of these if they don't get treated quickly.

A blizzard brings heavy snowfall and strong winds to Yellowstone National Park, Wyoming, USA.

In March 1993, a ferocious blizzard known as the 'Storm of the Century' hit the USA. Over a metre of snow fell in some places, burying cars and making roads impassable.

WHITE-OUT

The worst blizzards are white-outs where wind-blown snow makes it almost impossible to see. Because you cannot see the horizon or judge distances, it is easy to lose your bearings, so that you don't know where you are.

Iowa City, USA, in February 2011. As the wind picks up, a blizzard becomes a white-out and the horizon vanishes completely.

Europe has suffered unusually cold winters recently. Here, a snowplough clears the snow-covered streets of Berlin after a blizzard swept across Germany in January 2011.

CHILL FACTOR

One of the worst dangers of blizzards is the wind chill factor. This makes it feel colder than it actually is and the stronger the wind, the colder it feels. For example, if the temperature is 4ºC, and the wind speed is 48km/h, it can feel like -11ºC.

WIND CHILL	DESCRIPTION
0ºC to -10ºC LOW	It feels slightly uncomfortable outdoors. Warm clothing, a hat and gloves are recommended.
-10ºC to -25ºC MODERATE	Feels cold on uncovered skin. Hat, gloves and layers of warm clothing are necessary. Being outdoors for long periods can be dangerous.
-25ºC to -45ºC COLD	All skin must be covered. Move about to keep warm. Risk of hypothermia. Frostbite can occur very rapidly on uncovered skin.
-45ºC to -59ºC WARNING LEVEL	Dangerously cold. Outdoor activity should be limited to short periods. Severe risk of hypothermia. All skin should be covered with winter clothing. Exposed skin freezes in minutes.
-60ºC and colder VERY EXTREME	Conditions outdoors are extremely hazardous. High risk of hypothermia. Any exposed skin will freeze in two minutes. Stay indoors.

BLIZZARD SURVIVAL TIPS

1. Stay indoors, out of the cold. If the power goes off, stay in one room for warmth.

2. If you're caught outside, take shelter or dig a snow hole. A snow hole can trap heat, just like the walls of an **igloo**.

3. Stay hydrated by drinking water, but don't eat snow as it lowers your body temperature.

4. If you're caught in the car, don't get out and walk. Turn on the heater every few minutes, keeping a window open for fresh air. Tie something colourful to the car's aerial for rescuers to spot.

5. Wear layers of clothing. These will trap heat. Keep moving your arms and legs so that you stay warm.

FLOOD

Floods happen when water from rivers or the sea overflows areas that are usually dry land. Heavy rainfall can turn rivers into raging torrents, sweeping away everything in their path, while powerful storms can send giant waves of seawater inland – with catastrophic results.

WILD WATER

Floods are the worst type of wild weather. Each year they kill more people than any other natural disaster, including earthquakes and erupting volcanoes. Over the centuries, floods have claimed millions of lives.

A huge flood can be disastrous, sweeping away homes, roads, crops and cars. **Stagnant** floodwater can also spread disease. Despite the risks, hundreds of millions of people around the world live on floodplains (the flat land alongside rivers that gets covered with water when it floods). The main reason is that the rich soil in these areas is good for growing crops.

In the summer of 2010, monsoon rains caused catastrophic flooding in Pakistan, destroying 1.7 million homes. This picture shows people, surrounded by floodwater, being rescued by helicopter.

Survivors wade down a flooded road in central Pakistan during the August 2010 floods.

RIVER FLOODS

Melting snow or very heavy rain can cause a river to burst its banks and flood the surrounding land. The worst floods happen along the world's largest rivers, such as the Yangtze in China. In 1998, heavy **monsoon** rains caused floods that left 4,000 people dead and 15 million homeless.

FLASH FLOODS

Flash floods happen very quickly when heavy rain falls on a small area, such as a valley or gorge. The rainwater gets funnelled into a ferocious flow that can destroy everything in its path. Flash floods also happen in deserts where dry river beds can suddenly turn into raging torrents.

COASTAL FLOODS

Coastal floods occur when tsunamis (caused by earthquakes at sea) or violent storms raise the sea level so much that water sweeps inland. Most coastal floods are caused by tropical storms, such as hurricanes. These can cause a **storm surge**, raising the level of the sea by up to five metres.

FUTURE FLOODING

Climate change will make flooding more likely in some places. Sea levels are slowly rising, because of the melting polar ice caps and because the water in the sea expands as it warms. Higher sea levels make coastal flooding more likely during storms. Changes in climate could also mean heavier rains in some parts of the world, leading to more river floods and **flash floods**.

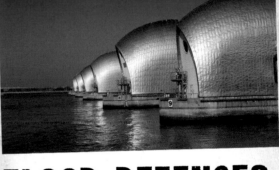

The flood barrier across the River Thames is a barrage that is closed to protect London from high tides and storm surges.

FLOOD DEFENCES

To protect against flooding, walls or embankments are sometimes built along riverbanks. These are called 'levees' (from the French word for 'raised') and are often built from soil covered in grass, gravel or concrete. Levees make the riverbank higher and stop water overflowing onto the floodplain.

Another type of flood protection is a barrage. This is a dam-like structure, built across a river estuary. Its gates are usually left open to let river water flow out to sea, but can be closed to stop storm surges moving back up the river to flood low-lying land.

SCORCHED EARTH

When a region suffers long spells of dry weather, a drought may happen. Without rain the soil becomes dry and cracked, while plants wither away and die. Even if some rain falls, there is not enough water to soak into the ground before it dries out again.

DEADLY DROUGHT

Droughts are a natural feature of the climate in many parts of the world, especially in places that normally have a low amount of rainfall. But they can be made worse by human activities, such as overfarming, cutting down large areas of trees or the over-use of water.

Droughts can last for months or even, in extreme cases, for years, with terrible results. Water is vital for life and water shortages can kill crops and animals. In poorer countries, droughts can lead to terrible famine, starvation and disease. Dry soil breaks up and is easily whipped up by the wind into dust storms. There is also a greater risk of **wildfires**.

Women queue for food in a **refugee camp** in Somalia. Severe drought in East Africa in 2011 has led to a devastating famine affecting Somalia, Ethiopia and Kenya.

Drought has dried up the water of this lake in South Australia, killing the trees along its shoreline.

HEATWAVES

A heatwave is a period of very hot weather that lasts much longer than usual. There may also be high humidity, so that it feels hot and sticky at the same time. Heatwaves can be deadly. In Australia, heatwaves have killed more than 4,000 people over the last hundred years, making them deadlier than any other natural disaster.

High temperatures can cause serious health problems, such as heat exhaustion and life-threatening heat stroke, but it is not just the heat that makes people ill. When the wind drops in cities, dirt and fumes hang in the air. This creates a choking fog of polluted air, called smog, making it hard to breathe.

A cloud of smog hangs over Los Angeles, USA. Smog can be a serious health hazard in large cities.

The 2003 heatwave led to drought and crop failures right across Europe.

HOTHOUSE EUROPE

In 2003, a heatwave hit Europe, bringing the hottest summer for 450 years. More than 40,000 people died; 15,000 in France alone. Some parts of France had temperatures above 40°C for a whole week. In southern Portugal, temperatures hit 48°C, causing forest fires to break out. Three years later, another massive heatwave hit Europe. Britain had its hottest July ever, with temperatures reaching 36.5°C.

WILDFIRE

Giant roaring wildfires can start from small beginnings. All it takes is a spark from a campfire during a hot summer's day and moments later, fire can be raging through the dry grass and trees. Flames can spread through a forest faster than a person can run, destroying everything they encounter.

HOW FIRES START

Fires always start with a source of heat. In remote areas of forests, where there are few people, the most common cause of wildfires is lightning. The huge electric current that passes through a tree hit by lightning can set the tree on fire. In areas where people live or visit, most wildfires are started accidentally, either by campfires, discarded cigarettes, or sparks from machinery or fallen power lines. Some wildfires are even started deliberately.

FAST FLAMES

Once a wildfire has started, it spreads along a line of burning vegetation called a flame front. The flame front burns everything in front of it, leaving smouldering ashes behind. Winds and the slope of the ground control how fast the fire moves. With a wind behind it, a flame front can advance more than two metres each second. Flames spread more quickly uphill than downhill.

The fiercest wildfires spring up where there is thick, super-dry vegetation. The burning is so intense that it sends hot air swirling high into the atmosphere, creating strong winds and even mini-tornadoes, called fire devils.

A flame front advances through the dry vegetation north of Los Angeles in the Station Wildfire of 2009.

WILDFIRE ZONES

Wildfires are most common in places that experience hot, dry summers, and where there is forest, scrubland or grassland. The world's wildfire hotspots are the west of North America and the south-east of Australia. In these areas, the summer is known as the 'fire season'. The hot weather dries out the vegetation, and warm, strong winds blow regularly. As the climate warms, many scientists expect that wildfires will become more common.

BLACK SATURDAY

In February 2009, the Australian state of Victoria was bone dry. No rain had fallen for months on end, and a record-breaking heatwave made conditions perfect for wildfires to start. On 7 February, strong winds toppled electricity power lines, starting many small fires. In the wind, they quickly grew into a massive wildfire that tore through the bush, engulfing several towns. In all, 173 people were trapped and killed by smoke and flames. The day became known as 'Black Saturday'.

Firefighters monitor the progress of the 2009 Station Wildfire as it approaches the city of Los Angeles, USA.

FIGHTING FIRE

Firefighters use different ways to stop a fire spreading, including clearing gaps in the forest that fire cannot cross, called firebreaks. These are made with bulldozers and hand tools. Firefighters can also drop chemicals called fire retardants from aircraft onto trees to slow down the spread of a fire. On the ground, firefighters use water hoses and beaters to try to put out flames.

A plane drops red fire retardant onto the trees to slow the progress of a wildfire in the south of France in 2006.

EARTHQUAKE

Earthquakes are among nature's most destructive forces, capable of flattening cities and killing or injuring thousands of people. Suddenly, the earth trembles and cracks, or lurches up and down, sending buildings crashing to the ground and burying streets, cars and people under rubble.

The 1995 earthquake in Kobe, Japan, caused the collapse of more than 200,000 buildings across the city.

EARTHQUAKE

The incredible force of an earthquake is now in your hands! Trigger different strength earthquakes and see the destruction caused.

SHOCKWAVES

Earthquakes happen when the tectonic plates of the Earth's crust jostle each other, putting the rocks under strain. Sometimes, the plates lock together, causing the forces to build up. Then they suddenly give way, releasing the pressure as an earthquake. Most earthquakes happen at plate boundaries, where deep cracks known as **faults** form in the Earth's crust.

The point deep underground where the rocks slip is called the hypocentre. From here, shockwaves of energy spread out through the ground. Directly above the hypocentre is the epicentre. This is the point on the surface where the earthquake's effects can be felt and seen.

NORMAL FAULT

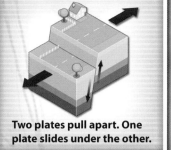

Two plates pull apart. One plate slides under the other.

REVERSE FAULT

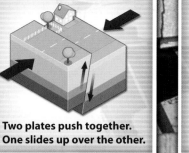

Two plates push together. One slides up over the other.

STRIKE SLIP FAULT

Two plates slide past each other in opposite directions.

Experts test an earthquake early-warning system, checking a seismograph screen for signs of shockwaves.

MEASURING QUAKES

Tens of thousands of earthquake tremors shake the Earth each year, but thankfully most are too small to be felt. About a hundred are strong enough to cause some damage, while around ten are seriously earth-shattering. Earthquake experts called seismologists use the Moment Magnitude Scale (MMS) to grade earthquakes. It measures the energy that is released by an earthquake on a scale from one to ten.

QUAKE PROOF

A major cause of death during earthquakes is collapsing buildings, so architects have been designing buildings that are better able to stand the shaking. One of the most famous quake-proofed buildings is the Transamerica Pyramid in San Francisco, USA. Its shape makes it very stable, plus it sits on underground rollers that let it rock gently.

The Transamerica Pyramid swayed during an earthquake in 1989, but it did not fall down.

TSUNAMI

An earthquake under the sea can trigger a tsunami – a series of giant waves that race across the sea. At first, the waves are low, but as they near land they slow down and build up to a great height. Then massive walls of water crash down on to the shore, washing people, buildings and vehicles away.

HOW A TSUNAMI HAPPENS

Tsunamis are usually caused by earthquakes under the sea. These cause a sudden shift in the seabed, forcing a huge volume of water upwards. Tsunamis can also be triggered by undersea volcanoes or landslides creating giant waves.

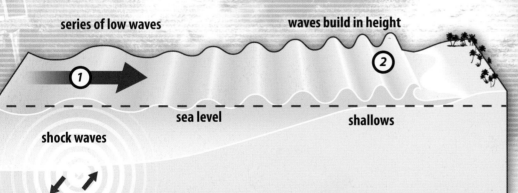

series of low waves

waves build in height

1

2

sea level

shallows

shock waves

1 The shock sets in motion a series of waves that race across the ocean at speeds of up to 950km/h – as fast as a jet plane. At this stage the waves are usually less than a metre high and may be hundreds of kilometres apart.

2 As the waves reach the shallow water by the shore, they slow down. The tops of the waves move faster than the bottoms, making them rise up to great heights before crashing down on to the shore.

A tsunami wave crashes over a street in Miyako City, Japan, after a massive earthquake struck in March 2011.

On 26 December 2004, a colossal 9.3 magnitude earthquake off the coast of Indonesia triggered a massive tsunami. Around 300,000 people died.

DEADLY WAVES

A huge wall of water isn't always the first sign of an approaching tsunami. If the trough (low point) between the wave crests reaches the coast first it pulls the water away from the shore, exposing the sea floor. This is an important warning sign – the waves may be less than five minutes away.

The danger does not pass with the first wave that hits land. It may be followed by many others, between 10 to 45 minutes apart. These follow-up waves can push the water at least one kilometre inland.

TSUNAMI WARNING

Most tsunamis happen in the Pacific Ocean. They are tracked by the Pacific Tsunami Warning Centre in Hawaii. A series of pressure sensors on the sea bed measure the weight of water above them. If a tsunami passes, the sensors send signals to a chain of buoys sitting on the surface. These beam the information to a satellite, which signals the alarm to an early warning centre.

AVALANCHE

With a gigantic roar, a huge slab of snow breaks loose and hurtles down a mountainside at high speed. Nothing can stop an avalanche in full flow. As it travels downhill, it gets even faster, burying everything in its path under thick snow: cars, buildings and whole villages. Escape is almost impossible.

SNOW MOTION

Avalanches occur when a mass of snow suddenly breaks loose and crashes down a mountainside. They are most common after a large fall of fresh, powdery snow. The snow piles up quickly, overloading the icy slab underneath and causing it to crack. This makes the soft snow above unstable and it starts to slip and slide. Many avalanches are triggered by the movements of walkers or skiiers, but lots of other things can set them off, including a gust of wind or a noise, such as a car door slamming.

RACE AGAINST TIME

Avalanches can race downhill at more than 300km/h, making them almost impossible to outrun. The chances of being rescued alive from an avalanche are low. The snow sets like concrete, making it impossible to move. Most people survive if they are dug out in 15 minutes. But after 45 minutes, only a quarter survive. Search and rescue teams have to work fast to find survivors and dig them out.

Rescue teams use long sticks called snow probes and specially trained dogs with sensitive noses to find survivors buried under the snow.

On 23 February 1999, a huge avalanche crashed down on the village of Galtür in the Austrian Alps, burying buildings and killing 31 people.

SNOW PROOF

In avalanche danger zones, various ways of reducing the risk have been tried. These include setting off explosives to deliberately trigger small, controlled avalanches, which prevents larger build-ups of snow.

Steel fences, nets, dams and bridges are often built in avalanche-prone areas and rows of trees are planted across mountain slopes to hold back any falling snow.

AVALANCHE SURVIVAL

* If you are going into an avalanche risk area, wear a rescue beacon that signals where you are.

* If you're caught in a snow slide, try to grab on to a rock or a tree.

* If you're being swept away, try to 'swim' to the surface.

* Close your mouth so that you don't swallow too much snow.

* If you're buried, keep one hand in front of your face to keep an air space free.

FUTURE FALLS

Although global warming may mean less snow, it could mean more avalanches. Higher temperatures in mountains could lead to more freeze-thaw cycles of snow. This creates an icy, slippery top layer so that new snowfall can slide easily downhill in an avalanche.

A huge avalanche crashes violently down the side of the mountain K2 in the Karakoram Range, Pakistan.

VOLCANO

An erupting volcano is a spectacular sight. Glowing rivers of molten rock, called lava, burst from beneath the Earth's crust, sometimes with terrifying explosive force. Towering clouds of ash and thick landslides of mud add to its devastating impact.

VOLCANO

Take a look inside a volcano and then make it blow its top in a violent and fiery eruption.

LETHAL LAVA

A volcano occurs at an opening in a weak spot of the Earth's crust, where molten rock, called magma, bursts or leaks out. When magma reaches the surface it is called lava. Different types of lava cause different types of eruption and form different shapes of volcano.

There are roughly 50 volcanic eruptions around the world each year, but the Earth has around 1,500 active volcanoes in total. About half of these can be found in an area around the Pacific Ocean called the 'Ring of Fire'. Volcanoes on land make up only about a third of all volcanoes. The rest occur under the sea.

The Soufrière stratovolcano on the Caribbean island of Montserrat violently erupted in 1997.

STRATOVOLCANO

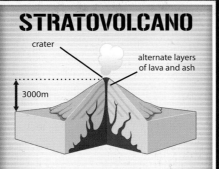

crater

alternate layers of lava and ash

3000m

SHAPE: Tall and symmetrical cone shape with steep sides.
MADE FROM: Alternate layers of thick lava and ash that have built up over centuries of eruptions.

CINDER CONE

layers of volcanic fragments

500m

SHAPE: Small, rounded cone shape with very steep sides.
MADE FROM: Cinders ejected in mild eruptions. Often found on the sides of other volcanoes.

SHIELD VOLCANO

old lava flows

new lava flows

5000m

central vent

SHAPE: Wide and low dome shape, with gently sloping sides.
MADE FROM: Thin, runny lava that flows for tens of kilometres before cooling and setting hard.

VOLCANIC HAZARDS

Lava flows: lava can reach temperatures of 1200°C and usually destroys everything in its path. However, it rarely kills people because it does not flow very fast.

Pyroclasts: these are rocks hurled out from volcanoes. The biggest are volcanic 'bombs' which can be fist-sized or bigger.

Ash clouds: an eruption can blast out huge quantities of ash. The ash travels on the wind, burying towns, fields and people when it falls.

Pyroclastic flows: these are lethal avalanches of ash and gas that flow down the sides of volcanoes at great speed. Anything caught up in them is destroyed.

Lahars: these are massive mudflows formed when volcanic ash mixes with water. They can sweep downhill for hundreds of kilometres before setting hard like concrete.

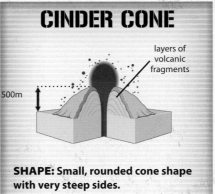

ASH CLOUD CHAOS

Eyjafjallajoküll (say: Ay-uh-fyat-luh-yo-kuut-lul) is a stratovolcano in Iceland. In March 2010, a series of small earthquakes warned that an eruption was likely. The volcano then erupted twice, creating a cloud of volcanic ash nine kilometres high. As the ash cloud spread over northern Europe it caused chaos, grounding planes and leaving air passengers stranded.

CLIMATE CHANGE

The Earth's atmosphere is slowly getting warmer. This change is called global warming. As the temperature rises, the world's climates are being affected. Many scientists believe that climate change is caused by human activities.

THE EVIDENCE

Weather records collected carefully for hundreds of years show us that the Earth's atmosphere is warming. Over the last hundred years its average temperature has increased by 0.8°C. This doesn't sound like a lot, but an increase of just a few degrees could have a devastating impact on our planet and its climate.

We can see some effects of climate change already. For example, the world's glaciers are slowly melting and the ice covering the Arctic Ocean is shrinking every year. Sea levels are rising, too. In the last century, they have risen between 10 and 25 centimetres. Patterns of rainfall are changing, with more rain falling in some places and less in others.

THE EFFECTS

Some people blame climate change for natural disasters, such as hurricanes and floods, but we can't be certain if it is the cause of individual weather events. However, climate change is likely to cause major problems in the future, especially if we do nothing to stop it.

Climate change could make floods, blizzards and droughts more common. Changes in temperature and rainfall could affect crops, causing drought and famine in the drier areas of the world. A rise in sea level could have the greatest impact, affecting millions of people. Low-lying coastal areas, such as Bangladesh, would be flooded more regularly and many coastal cities would become uninhabitable.

Climate change and the melting of the polar ice caps could affect the survival of many creatures, such as polar bears.